D0442846

)

19

HYBRIDA

HYBRIDA

POEMS

TINA CHANG

W. W. NORTON & COMPANY

Independent Publishers Since 1923 ★ New York London

For information about permission to reproduce selections from this book, write to
Permissions, W. W. Norton & Company, Inc., 500 Fifth Avenue, New York, NY 10110

For information about special discounts for bulk purchases, please contact
W. W. Norton Special Sales at specialsales@wwnorton.com or 800-233-4830

Manufacturing by Versa Press
Book design by Lovedog Studio
Production manager: Julia Druskin

Library of Congress Cataloging-in-Publication Data

Names: Chang, Tina, author.
Title: Hybrida : poems / Tina Chang.
Description: First edition. | New York : W. W. Norton & Company, [2019]
Identifiers: LCCN 2018056723 | ISBN 9781324002482 (hardcover)
Subjects: LCSH: United States—Race relations—Poetry. | American poetry—21st century.
Classification: LCC PS3603.H3574 A6 2019 | DDC 811/.6—dc23
LC record available at https://lccn.loc.gov/2018056723

W. W. Norton & Company, Inc., 500 Fifth Avenue, New York, N.Y. 10110
www.wwnorton.com

W. W. Norton & Company Ltd., 15 Carlisle Street, London W1D 3BS

1 2 3 4 5 6 7 8 9 0

FOR JULIETTE & ROMAN

CONTENTS

HE, PRONOUN

Everywhere I look I see him,
I have a right to fear for him,

though I have no right to claim his color.
His blackness is his to own and what will

my mouth say of that sweetness.
Am I colorless worn like a veil, invisible

but present. He is a word grown upright
and some claim he is journalism, media

around me, so much light filtered through,
so much video of him, I shut it out,

the body shot through and I will not let
him out the door. Sideways, I view

a lens. If you could see the green field,
the cows with their maternal gazes, instinct

at their hooves, leaning into calves, edging in.
They come closer. When there is no more color,

I turn an old-fashioned knob of the TV,
black-and-white frames, where I view a hose

releasing water, dogs bark at the leash of time.
My son turns off the television believing it's an ancient

toy. He sits on my lap and we lean against a wall,
he and I in the room. We watch the door.

CREATION MYTH

~ Origin ~

I'm without body but forming in the latticework

      of blood cell and fret. Each threat pulls me upward

tempting and building me until my spine lifts into a column,

      a kingdom. I can imagine life shaped as God-self,

a fortress grows beyond me. Seeing into that distance, I glow.

      The heart begins first in sound like footsteps up a staircase,

the curled fist knocks for entrance, the heart courses

      into garnet-being heavier than matter, lighter than flame.

I find shape, I shift from spirit and my lungs heave with gravity,

      float into the presence of air. I wonder if my mother

is summoning me. Isn't that her song parting the curtains,

      isn't that the cry that opens the shutters?

She says *changeling, become a boy.* Once I was a dream animal

      running. I knew there was something larger than me calling

and I ran after it like prey, as if I knew it had to be mine. I salivated,

seized by a charge, I wondered. My mind rose into a volcano,

molten heat surged like the ire of my future. I am now searching

for my mother to find completion slick as sound,

rough as water, I am scaling, sniffing for utterance, a timber,

a lost call, howling at the stars, and my eyes, bright diamonds

with which to see by, my mouth, these rough shores I invite you to walk.

When I'm large enough will you recognize me?

I am your son. I never found any form to be truer.

I am fighting to be alive, fighting to be one.

~

Beyond is a voice and it says:
There is a car and the door is about to open.

There is a voice and it answers:
And destruction is pointed at the boy of history.

The future is the shadow of a boy, arms raised
whose eyes widen toward bloom as they stand:

two bodies of struggle. The officer believes
the instrument's sermon, believes the gun

is fueled when he shines it. Color the cloth violence.
He buffs the bright cylinder from which the bullet

will emerge and points it toward a future intention.
Color the cloth vengeance for it has no true name.

Are justice and victory the same laurels?
The world spins mindful of its past.

I envision, now, my son rising, arms above him,
like hosanna out of a car.

See https://www.youtube.com/watch?v=mu8ypoNyzrw

~

Born

Birth

Birthright

Right

Birth son

Son at the right hand of the father

"It was 1 a.m. and Michael Brown Jr. called his father, his voice trembling. He had seen something overpowering. In the thick gray clouds that lingered from a passing storm this past June, he made out an angel. And he saw Satan chasing the angel and the angel running into the face of God."

Is poetry proof of evidence? says one student.
If so, wouldn't we be assuming there is a guilty party?
    says another student.

~

I walked the night searching for my father's approval.
I arrived at his funeral, my belly heavy not with burden
but with the weight of his absence.

I searched for him the way a gull searches for a tide
whose fury carries it across years. When it lands
it heaves with the breathless knowledge of oceans.

Now my son can see. Now his lips have formed.
Now he hears me. When my son was born, his cry
fell into a well. There was a ripple in the water

whose rings circle out to infinity.
It fashions its own pattern of luck and light.
I anointed my son: *one who lives without ancestors,*

apart from the pride.

~

Hosanna

In the New Testament, Christ arrives
in Jerusalem and is hailed as the *Deliverer*.
Translated from Hebrew Hosanna means
"save now," a petition to be set free.
When the multitudes spread palm branches
before Christ, they recognized him as the King
who would free them from bondage.

~

I named him Roman after lost empires
frozen in time to their historical might.
Roman, imagined horses surging,
racing toward a colossal urge,
a triumph which has no name.
Roman, nothing could touch him.
Nothing could harm him, his name
a shield, a circle of fire surrounding him
in which nothing, no authority, no will,
no gun, no warring cacophony
of insurgence, no charging
battalion could touch him.

Roman sounds like *run* if uttered quickly,
for the towering structure he will be.
Roman, warrior. Roman Ren.
Ren, after my own father who died
too soon. Ren, a brother to many men.
Roman, I yell after him when I see him
on his bicycle riding too far from me.
I yell after him, again and again.
Roman, Roman, Roman. He can't hear me.

"The only way I learned about him was from a guy calling me on my phone. I was able to look on his phone and say that is my son lying in the streets for hours. Hours."

—Lesley McSpadden, mother of Michael Brown

~

There are portraits on the wall, ones of self-identification.
In kindergarten, his teacher lays out the colors
they'll use for their portraits. Her hand touches
a leaf of paper and she names it mocha. Another
hand on a page she claims is umber. Chosen.
Branded. From of a stack of construction paper
my son picks a color for his face. Gleeful,
he works with scissors awkwardly making
what he believes to be a replica. He cuts
large waves for hair and pastes it atop
the oval head, Elmer's glue seeps from the undersides
of paper. When he is done, he tears a large red swath
which is the mouth curled into joy. No teeth,
just lips turned up into a grin like a boat afloat at sea.

~

Hunter

The face in darkness is on the verge of vanishing.
He's swallowed by a growing furnace of a mouth.

He's been having night visions
where the self eats the self.

The officer wakes to this vision the morning
of the hearing and when he is questioned his face

is flushed. He remembers to use words that will make
Michael Brown seem threatening: *Make him the hunter.*

Make the boy the hunter. I will be the prey.
In the fairy tale, the hunter disappears by story's end.

~

In a future story, they bound through grasses.
I continue the fairy tale, the one where the forest
grows thick with worry. I grow old and slim
with worry. This is how it will be told: I starve

in the forest with concern. I thin to sliver thinking
of all my boys. They are night syrup, they are earth,
all of my sons so hungry with me. We drink
from the lake, unsure what's beyond the mountain.

When I wake, the nurses hold my ankles
and hands. My mind moves my son's
engine body to me as he slowly
crawls up my chest, searching for me.

~

For all that we say about death and its peace
and its privacy, it is better to live. Up ahead,
the mountain strikes the sky with its crown.
When my son arrives ahead of me, I follow him
to pasture, running after footsteps of erasure.
The siren wails and reminds me the city
is a living creature who waits outside
the periphery.   Panting.

PATIENCE

I come from gravel falling from the mouth, a bent spine
from which my mother rose, from the sickness that poured
over my father in water buckets. That was the well he fell into
and the well where I waited, a body cutting into water on impact.

My face is the only heirloom, fixed in gold. The features
which swirl down a drain. I come from that too, not sewage
nor explosion but a phantom lock, a combination set
to be opened. A slap in the dark. A gun goes off.

I come from the story of chicken breeders, of nurses, of railroad,
bone soup, chopping block, the work of chopping, then finally food.
I come from handmade shirts hanging in my stepfather's closet.
I come from the spit and curses that careened from his mouth

like anvils and vespers. Lamps unlit, medicine, tubes,
worn flags, failing lungs making up an American song
in each room of the house. I come from stickball bat
and missing bases, empty trailer in the lot across the street,

light that flickered on and off signaling one lone presence.
I come from the broad birds and the day demons, the ash
from a childhood burn, tin cans of dried pens, newspaper,
seashells, a phoenix fixed in a souvenir bottle. Every bit saved

as if discard were memory itself. As if I lived on paper, a breeze.
I come from wayward bicycle, departure through a heavy door,
a forklift, a lion's claw, a den of starving wolves. I am frantic
running through the house, closing shutters, hiding silverware.

I am found in my bed, breathing. I come from a dead end
that opened toward the brick face of a horizon which glowed
like God's goat face, a wild compassion, a guttural sound
from the throat. I come from the last funeral, my stepfather

in a casket with all the living flowers, his hands sewn
together in death though I remember in life they raged
punctuating each hungry vowel. How the orchids
overwhelmed his body, his poisonous face. Face

of my past. I come from that too, from the indifference
of doors and keys, from the sonnet of the sewing machine
which wrestled my neck at the collar and all my words
caught at the throat, struggled to make one stitch, a straight line.

I come from those birds: heron, robin, grackle.
The ones you cannot catch. The ones that sound
like owls or witches. I come from the rough seas of this sort
of battle, of consequences all too familiar and fantastic.

I gulp the world's water, salt with rage, froth with effort.
I come from that, the flailing struggle, my afterlife waiting for me,
and a future summoning at my ankles. The future is an animal
waiting to pounce. It is that bestial. That patient.

I come from that, too.

SHE, AS PAINTER

I sing a song to my children.
If I sing it just right, it is greater
than a psalm. It is a hilltop.
It is thunder. My daughter finds me
in the bed sleeping, she places
her head to my chest.

One beat. A leap. Slow listening.
When my stepfather was alive
judgment was beast inside his mouth.
When he died, I was relieved.
No more of his laughter beside me
at the childhood table. No more slaughter.

My daughter worries and shakes me awake.
Until I reassure her my living
is living inside her too.
I place her in the bed with me
where she sinks into the mattress.
I dream her fear and dream her safety

simultaneously slithering down
a tree. I smooth down the curls
of her hair, the waves of which
are now holding up a boat.
We sit together bobbing.
She feels she has painted

the sky's complication.
We are changed by their hue,
and their shifting lumen. I can't take
this love I feel. The waters rise up
and I assure her the water will not spill
into the boat. Water teeters at the edge.

MANKIND IS SO FALLIBLE

We lie down to the day as if we could flee
from the body's burden. On the ground are notes,
candles, a saint's face painted alive with gold.

Where does God live if not in the shadows
of struggle, marching next to the living,
with battlements and a slogan, knowing

faintly more than we do? Someone dispatches
a call for help. Someone notes the patches
on a man's jacket. Somewhere there is a circle

of people praying and dying at once, the loss
of which makes a narrative rain down
in news feeds across frames of light.

~

My mother once gave up her savior,
walked into our living room to profess
her love for the here and now.

She no longer believed in the unseen,
could no longer bow to invisible idols.
She sat on the chair in front of me

more mortal than she ever was,
face lit with resolve, done with faith,
done with the promise of rapture.

Somewhere, glass breaks
and the one who shatters it
wears a mask of God's many faces.

~

How would the body be summoned
if we started over? Imagine a blank book
in which the body is drawn.

Would the body lie horizontal like a violin
whose music plays off-key or would it stand
upright like a totem pole against its own weather?

I place a book under my pillow
as the ancient Japanese courtesans did
to dream the body into being.

Wind gathers from the past until I am walking
in snow. The arms and legs move in unison
with the mind, an engine of sinew and meat.

How should I draw it, not the body
but what it contains. Not its contours
but its tensions. Not its stew of blood

and clattering bones but its promise.
I prefer now to think of the body's debt
and what it owes to the ledger of the living.

~

I imagine the courtesans rising from sleep,
hair rushing to the waist like ink. They rub
their eyes of dream, tighten their robes

as they lift the book from beneath their pillow
as if urging a stone from its bedrock.
How would they think of the body then,

having wakened from that place
one could describe as near death.
Instead, the body startles forward toward infinity.

~

The courtesan runs her hand along the page,
feels the blank space, an urgent bell summons her.
Dips her brush in ink and draws a line through emptiness.

When a young man enters a church,
he seeks a furnace to burn away his hatred
and a foundation on which to kneel.

He seeks his mother's mercy
and his father's vengeance. He passes through
the doors and we call this worship.

If it could be as simple as sleep, curling inward
toward an avalanche of hummingbirds, the mind
freeing itself as the body lets go its earthly wreckage.

If it could be like enduring the wholeness of a dream
so real we dissolve into a veil of the past,
wind dragged backward, so brutal in its disappearance.

MILK

Milk in the batter! Milk in the batter! We bake cake!
And nothing's the matter!
     —Maurice Sendak, IN THE NIGHT KITCHEN

In every definition of home, my son conjures
milk. The sun as milk, milk spills through open
doorways, bed of warm milk, face of milk,
milk trousers, a truck full of milk. A milky light
passes through the lens of my camera.

All of his young life, my son thought of milk,
and he asked for it each night. In every memory
I have of him, his hands are outstretched
and he is asking for his last bottle.
In every version of a life, I never refuse him.

On the television, the nation listens to the story
of Leiby Kletzky. Today, I think of his mother
who waited for him, allowing him for the first time
to walk home alone. That morning, he held a key,
heavy and shining, made especially for him.

In the ancient story of boys, he headed up
the street past the lone dog barking near
the fire hydrant, past the circle of children
careening into their own shadows.
In the ancient story of boys, he walked through

his front door and this was his rite of passage.
He placed his book bag on the coffee table,
and the boy and the mother sat together
in the large reading chair, in the living room light.
But this version isn't true.

Tonight, I hold my son closer. As I put on his night
clothes, I'm afraid of the world. I find all the stories
horrifying. In the book of nursery rhymes the old woman
sends her son to bed without food, a king beats
a knave for stealing pies, and the dog cannot find his bone,

though he runs in circles day after day. Perhaps
if I rewrite all the old stories, a new era will begin.
Era of the Forgiven. Era of Redemption. Era
of Safekeeping. Tonight milk stains my blouse,
love so deep, it runs from me. After the old stories

are finished, my son says, *The story, again*. I open
the book. The owls lift from the pages. The lake
is a bowl of night milk. And this, a place so safe,
we are weightless, buoyant in its murky sweetness.
Free from a promise that each new day startles us alive.

REVOLUTIONARY KISS

I had never created man before so I invented my son first as a dream body. In order to create the dream body I must first believe in the force of opposites, a terrible tension of what has existed and the struggle yet to come. And it is true, that I had a notion of him for many years; for generations my imagination traveled in search of him.

It seems unlikely that a kiss would have roots in the Haitian Revolution, but it does. Over a century ago, an uprising of hundreds of thousands of slaves freed themselves from chain and rope, from whip and guillotine, from bondage through the struggle of blood. They fought for thirteen years in a revolution to stand on the shores of their own land, newly named Haiti, as free people and they kissed the ground however damp with the blood of their mothers, fathers, brothers, and sons. Slaves, newly liberated, whispered my son's name, his body envisioned there, beneath the rust of shackles, beside shards of slaveowners' homes, rising with smoke from burned plantations. Past the pinnacle of scoured light, past the canopy of trees dripping with the uprising of future leaves, my son begins his journey to me.

Once there was a chain of kisses as my mother said goodbye to her brothers and sisters lined in a row, as she left Taiwan for America, a shock of leis around her neck as she waved to a country of ghosts. Her history was equally complex. She left China in 1949, before communists led by Chairman Mao took over mainland China. My mother crowded into a boat that would take her to the coast of Taiwan known as *the beautiful island*, which she would one day yearn to leave.

By foot, by boat, by train, by bus, by plane. It seems impossible these two histories intertwine so that one day I may find a dream body housed inside mine. All along, I wring my hands and worry, will I know how to mother him? What language will I speak? What will my mother utter once she discovers the detour of my ancestry? Will she abandon me, turn the portraits of my ancestors toward the wall, backs directed away from my longing?

When I woke, the doctor's voice was muffled and thick. My mind moved in syncopated pulses and I pushed until all energy drained and my body cracked open. Liquid gold rushed away. Finally and now. He arrived, a purpled creature, violet and squirming, face crushed into an emperor's expression.

Born from the urgency of immigrants, how futile all of my years of worrying. I should have known my boy would row his small boat to me, regardless of the sky above that shook down its lightning, and even if the ground was bruised and famished of fruit and even freedom, he would continue on as if a force were lulling him to bedrock. Right here between his eyebrows, there is a swell of light, a country where I belong, no longer a stranger to my own skin. My mouth to his temple, an alarm cries. Tanks roll through the tale squeaking, turning their heavy wheels. When I kiss him, history's weapons fall from my pockets, shields cast beneath attalea trees. I will now end my days of resistance, my lips searching the entirety of his dream face made mortal, my lost shadows now migrating in unison.

FURY

My son rubs his skin and names it brown,
his expression gleeful as I wipe a damp cloth
over his face this morning. Last night,
there were reports that panthers were charging
through the streets. I watched from my seat
in front of the television, a safe vista.
I see the savannah. Sometimes, though,
my son wakes to a kind of nightmare.
He envisions words on the wall and cannot
shake them. He tries to scratch them away
or runs out of the room but the words follow him.
None of it makes any sense but it's the ghost
of his fear that I fear.

What is a safe distance from the thoughts
that pursue us and what if the threat persists
despite our howling? Buildings collapse,
a woman falls down the stairs and lands
on her back, with only one eye open, half
awake to her living damage. I think
my son senses what is happening
on the street, his heart fiercely tethered
to mine. I know the world will find him
and tell him the history of his skin.
Harm will come searching for him
and pour into him its scorching mercury,
its nails, its bitter breath against his boyhood
skin still smelling of milk and wonder.

Somewhere, the panthers are running
starting fires fueled by a distinct hunger.
Somewhere there is a larger fire, a pyre
stoked by the fury of all that we have come
to understand, all that we could have done
but did not. Its flames lick the underside
of the earth. It propagates needing
only a frenzy of air to fan it to inferno.
I'll call that the Forest. The deep woods
are ahead and if the panthers could just reach it.
If I told you that all of this happens at night,
you wouldn't believe me. If I told you
all of this happens in the future, always
the future you would continue following
the scent you could only describe as smoke.
I'll call that Justice.

But aren't we talking about mercy and its dark
twin? Isn't that what's pummeling history
in the side as I write this? Isn't it the thorn
and the taser? Isn't it the chokehold
and the gold arm of vengeance? I say it
from my mouth and when it spills forth
it lands on the ground in a pool of light
reflecting back at me the one true blasphemy:

Love and love and love and love and
love and love and love and love and love
and love and love and love and love and
love and love and love and love and love
and love and love and love and love and
love is crowding the street and needs only air
and it lives, over there, in the distance burning.

hybrid (n.)

c. 1600, "offspring of plants or animals of different variety
or species," from Latin *hybrida*, variant of *ibrida* "mongrel,"
specifically "offspring of a tame sow and a wild boar," of
unknown origin but probably from Greek and somehow related
to *hubris*. A rare word before the general sense "anything a
product of two heterogeneous things" emerged c. 1850.

HYBRIDA: A ZUIHITSU

Once, the past was in dialogue with the future, a hybrid form. The origin of the word *hybrida* is Latin, from *ibrida*, or 'mongrel'—a creature of mixed breeds. Open interpretation of violence, collision of selves, histories, and languages. Is language a movement of spirit expressing itself through an outward mutation? I was born in America, contributing to a long line of mixed culture, crossed boundaries, the collaborative and combustible nature of words. If I grew up with dual language, dual identity, how can anything feel unified?

The fragmentation of the zuihitsu welcomes randomness, collage, a piecing (and piercing) of memory and imagination that adds up to a feeling akin to liberation. The liberation of imagination is the body's response to dominance and containment. To build, speak, and write a way through each darkness. Zuihitsu, erasure, reimagined ekphrastic poems, words in movement, journalism in conversation with invented narrative, fairy tales fused with the lyric imagination, language in dialogue with visual art—much of it isn't entirely new, but now, written with a singular hand, calls to me. I think of discomfort, creating spaces where one is uneasy in order to change.

Immigrant body, female body, mother body.
Is the creative body inherently vulnerable?
Damaged body. Dream body. Fluid body. Boy body.

~

During a panel discussion about hybrid forms at Sarah Lawrence College, Aracelis Girmay described the present generation as made up of not two arms, but multiple appendages, like octopuses. She was careful not to say octopi. That wasn't quite the word she envisioned as she held out her arms as if to touch something multi-limbed, iridescent.

In the same discussion, Rachel Zucker said, "Motherhood is a hybrid form and there haven't been enough discussions about this language." This utterance struck me: lexicon of mother, collage of maternal self, fusion of artistic forms made manifest through the lens of protection. But this language is often ignored, buried, dismissed, or dismantled. Mangled by teeth. An entire landscape of language.

Raising a boy who is black and Asian in this country, I've come to terms with the fact that I never truly confronted the full spectrum of race in my past, at least not enough. Race was never a vessel but a land that bled into the tide. It surged, carried me, and then I arrived at my body. I try not to cast my own identity aside to understand my son's. Sometimes, I feel my old self fading away. I attempt to hang on and let go at once. Sometimes when the room is populated, I search the borders for my own disappearance.

Anyone who has ever been born of mixed race feels this inheritance. Often, gestured as an in-between state, it is more like reaching for a bottomless depth. I sit before an illustration in a children's book by Jostein Gaarder called *Questions Asked*. The illustration by Akin Düzakin shows a self and what seems to be a shadow-self diving into the depths of water. It feels like this: questions with no end. If one lives within this feeling, it doesn't provide comfort but being. The diving down does not come without breathlessness: Fathomless foundation of questions, and a wooden trunk filled with more gleaming questions.

Perhaps there is a world down there.

~

By raising a boy, do I understand what it means to live as a black boy? How do I speak of his existence without appropriating his existence? I return to the language of mothers.

~

At a reading, I discussed childbirth and raising a black son. I was told that someone in the audience Googled, "Tina Chang and Black Son." I don't think anyone will find any information anywhere about this except in my poems. It's not Google-able, Google searched or defined: my son found within a search engine. When he was born, our mutual exhaustion was a hybrid sound.

Media can obliterate a spirited word (world).

I am not the same person I was. Time changes forms.

&

I write a long poem that focuses on a boy who rises from his beginnings in the womb and lives in a body made vulnerable by authorities. There are clippings, quotes, evidence which speak toward the poems that surround them. The fragmented form like zuihitsu has a place here. How can we make sense of chaos? What is the form for that?

Google-able fact: "Unarmed black people were killed at five times the rate of unarmed whites in 2015" (*Mapping Police Violence*).

Google-able fact: "There is no federal database that tracks the number of people of any race killed by police. Some individuals and groups have compiled their own databases, such as The Root and Hiphopandpolitics.com, using information from media and law enforcement reports" (*Los Angeles Times*).

Non-Google-able fact: When my son wakes from his dream, he finds me in another room folding clothes. He lies down next to me on the sofa. In his dream we are separated. There is an elsewhere, he says, where children sleep and never wake. I touch his forehead which now feels hot with fever.

&

List of the times my son has registered hurt:

- His friend kicks him in the spine. The mother of the boy does not notice.
- A neighbor asks him if he has a gun in his hoodie pocket.
- He walks up to a group of boys in his class. Turns back to me, asks me to say goodbye one more time.
- He mentions under his breath that I never listen to his stories.
- When I defend him from other boys too fiercely, he storms away. Slams the door.
- A white boy steals his school snacks and he is hungry. When he tells a head teacher, she doesn't believe him.

- My mother calls his hair crazy. She asks me to cut it each time she sees him.
- My friend tells me that all the girls like the blonde, blue-eyed boy in the class. When I'm silent she says, "They like your boy too, of course."
- The owner of the convenience store asks me if my children are my own. I say, "Yes, they are." She looks them up and down and demands, "Where is their father?"
- I ask him to get out of bed. Instead, he stands on his mattress and raises both arms up.
- Outside his window, he views police officers surround a man. He doesn't know if he should feel for the officers or the man standing at the center, panting hard.
- He often tells me he doesn't understand the meanness of boys. Mentions maybe it's better to stand somewhere in the middle or somewhere alone.
- In the basement of my home, his friend straddles him, punches him in the head over a dozen times. He does not sound out or call for help. Later, he said my husband told him never to hit a girl so he lay there waiting for the punches to stop.
- I was far from the house.
- I was not home.

~

I sometimes try not to register his pain. When I do, I often find myself immobile.

~

Hybrid forms leave fences open. They are wide fields with snow leopards, wolves, and honey bees. The combustion of imaginings form a lake, water spreading, explosions on the surface of an oil slick.

Hybrida is the change of properties. Long ago the earth plates shifted, came together in new permutations. New land. New World. It permits a space to be wounded, sutured, broken again, and untied to float to a beyond.

What lingers sounds like leaves crushed beneath feet, or the light that remains on after you're certain you've shut it, the house in the field over there, the one that keeps living whether you view it or not. Lights in the upstairs room. Shadows move when the wind changes its mind. It seems inhabited, doesn't it?

~

I am afraid for vocabulary and its presence in the struggle. It lives at the center of a circle and it's been bred to salivate, primed for impatience, with a hand at its back coaxing it toward its gritty death. This hand may be history but this is questionable. Vocabulary is the future we've all been waiting for. It lunges at the throat of man's deepest intentions. I hear the crush of cartilage, an ankle wobble for recovery, the quick intake of breath. There is a fall but the crowd is so thick now, I cannot see. I rely on my other senses to brace myself for what's about to happen.

~

Look out and look backward. The story we are living now is an ancient one. It has been lived before but feels new in this present existence. Open the books. This already happened, in veiled guises, on the shores of other lands, evolved forms hemorrhaged before they sprouted new wings, before the beak broke through the surface, a new oration, legs jutted from a rush of nomadic longing. Hybrida's translation: Wilderness of the mind. But it's changing.

LONG SHADOW

My daughter runs dragging a shadow of a blue dress. Her Mary Janes click behind me like a dove's lament. When we cross the street, I feel something give underfoot and see I've stepped on the beak of a small bird. We stoop to have a closer look and see another infant bird, then another, and another. I count five infant birds, the beginnings of feathers still wet from birth, flattened on the sidewalk. I look up and see a robin on a lamppost chirping above. I say, *That's the momma. I think her babies fell from a nest we can't see.* My daughter squinting upward says, *The momma doesn't seem sad. She's singing.*

~

My mother woke each morning, threatened by grit and mortality. Her slippers moved across the wood floor, scrape of dishes, a door opened then closed, and she was gone. The scent of death lingered behind her, my father the ghost, sat at the kitchen table. My brother and I raised ourselves. It was the first day I held the key my mother had made for me. I was alone and walked the six blocks home from school and could feel a sting in my belly. I tried to open the door as quickly as I could, the keys jangled clumsily in my grip. I couldn't set the key straight into the lock's opening. Warm liquid pooled down my stocking. The day was hot and my face stung. When inside, I took my stockings off and placed them in the trash can, burying them underneath paper tea cups and napkins, hoping my mother wouldn't find them. I placed the key back in a small pocket of my backpack. To keep it safe.

~

My daughter backed away from the birds and we continued our walk toward the park. I asked if we should get a shovel from home and bury the birds, the way I had buried something long ago when death once found me. She said, *I don't want to put them in the ground. I'm afraid.* The robin above chirped frantically. I stepped somewhere beneath the robin's shadow and disappeared.

~

When my daughter was very young I woke her often to make sure she was alive.

~

From the top bunk of my bed I sometimes thought I saw my father's long shadow in the hallway, turning a corner, his strange music moving from kitchen to living room. How many ways and for how many years did I recall his form? How do I place the pieces together, the rummaging is futile and familiar. I'm lost in the recollection of someone I knew before my origin. *Once Upon a Time* it happened once, never to repeat again. *Upon*: on the surface of, gliding, on top of, above, hovering, a palimpsest but long gone. *Time* as in never before, soon, very soon, and always into the future and back again. If you can imagine this, then you can enter the fairy tale. You have the key.

EVERY GRIMM

Dark gathers and climbs a hallowed tree.
Why does the running water gurgle,
cupped hands to dry mouth? The spring
is a tiger, tearing thirst to pieces.

The water is a wolf. The deer is a primal
thirst, face plunging downward to quench
its thick hunger, dangling with the insistence
of rain. The face softens, limbs totter

beneath the thrown fawn. A body fresh
and pale, rising from the lake's edge.
Sister, what is eating from your hand?
Brother, you were never human.

Why did you speak as a deer
when you were really a ghost?

STORM

I summon them. *Eat, children, eat.*
And they do. *Lie down, children,*
lie down. Though the sounds
of wolves move in the bushes,
they lie down. This is the trust they live,
the only one they sleep in. I falter,
I do not falter. Each day I live like this.
When I wake, the faces have fallen
off the wall. Small masks, a spell there.
My hands open to summon the children.
Come children, come, let's drift
beneath the table. The clouds shift
and change the face of the sky.
The planes fly past us. Let's lie
on our backs. Let's watch until
we feel the world turn beneath us.
Come children, let's gather
our things, let's find a hiding place
before the great storm comes.

ASTROTURF

Before my son was born, I had been inside my home often and, one spring day, sat myself on the astroturf behind a playground close to my home. I lay back, allowing the plastic grass to prick me on my arms and wrists. A few feet away, three girls sang a string of songs about love, heartbreak, all the while the lyrics broke and remade themselves on the edge of each spring leaf. I listened and I didn't listen at once which felt like my fullest attention. Each of the girls was so casual in their beauty, legs entangled in one another, fingers braiding each other's teen hair. They seemed like one animal of burnished light and I tried not to stare. It was the kind of beauty that held its own attention, needed no validation, long eyelashes and pale, long arms gestured toward wholly bright selves. I closed my eyes hearing their laughter. I heard, too, from afar a boy approaching. I heard a small thud as he sat down somewhere near them. They talked, they joked, and then a silence that made me open my eyes. After a longer pause, they asked him to please leave. I now saw the boy was black and I registered an expression that was slow rain coming down hard as he grabbed his backpack swinging it so fiercely, it almost hit one of the girls. As he walked away, they laughed past him. Their laughter was the long shadow that followed him for years, their laughter forced him to round the corner, almost gone from view. And before he disappeared, he yelled, "Bitch," but the memory of him left not a trace. No one told the girls to rethink their cruelty, no thorns left in their hair to remind them of the poison in their song. When I sat up, I felt a strong kick inside me. My boy would be here soon. Six more days into the future I would meet him. I touched the area that moved. I waited.

OBEDIENCE, AUTHORITY

It is wolf when the teeth bite down.
To say it is blue is too blue
to mention, for all of us privy
to the fall of history.

If it charges, the young ones
get it first, a shot,
a tear at the knee, flesh root
and no one knows

who is prey first
who is arm and leg,
broken spine,
the movement too quick,

the question always who
runs toward or away,
whose eyes are aimed
at the starting point, origin

a hole in a canopy of trees
where the highway veers off
when the wolf is netted,
it howls beneath the webbed

rope. It chews at its hind paw.
It finds it difficult to die
on its side with the alive eye
watching, centered on the blue.

The other eye moves beyond
sunlight and rifle pointed down,
boots with tongues unfurled
mud-filled. Gurgling.

BOY WITH PAVEMENT, A PAINTING

His eyes are two moons: one white, one black
sailing beside each other. The moons watch

backward viewing a past they can never
revise, clocks shine down on the boy on pavement.

Hole, what are you but the moon, carved from worry, muscled
out, and what is it but a zero of order, outline which resembles

nothing of the love his mother summoned to make a human
new. The soul can be a terrible spectrum of bones.

There are those who believe they are living gods,
a fiendish pack. They no longer hold a whip but the fist is ancient.

Each year, there are instruments of force moving
like lonely tides. Each new moon, the spirit of the boy

rises from pavement, walks to something impossible:
a lake beaming under a catastrophe of stars.

There is the smell of new grass when he stands
waist deep in water. I have not forgotten the moon

nor the phantom that rode beside it like a carriage
pulled by an intention of horses. If there are dual forces,

one moon was absorbed by the sky's tension,
one moon was symmetrical. Free.

4 PORTRAITS

after Henri Cole

Napoleon Leading the Army over the Alps, Kehinde Wiley

I never dreamed myself to be any larger
than a horse. Perhaps this is strange,
my girl body in the body of a man
on a rapturous equestrian animal. I am
not like the others. This was the song I sang
since my birth, since I had a mouth
to sing it. So I said it for years until I believed
jewels fell out of my mouth. Oh son,
I believe the mighty shall come.
I shall be a mother whose bright milk runs
with fever and anguished love, with a head
in my hands if the head shall equal justice.
I shall be a father too, glorious and eternal.

I shall be, for you, the man ascending the cliff
until the steed I ride throws me into the pasture
of the everlasting. If this is blasphemy
let me love the world into fantastic horses,
ride them to a distant country where I drown
in brocade, fragrant vine. If I am captured,
let my kingdom be laced in mega gold.
Let my cage be a godly frame.

go run tell dat, Alexandria Smith

If I am a girl in a traffic of legs, let them be trees.
If I am a mouth, let there be a chorus
of raucous tongues. If I set sail, let it be along a tide
of ribbons ebbing toward the widest America.
Let there be hair, each strand running along a road,
braided, and rebraided until what remains is glory.
Each face I wear leads to another face
and within that a sister. If I could multiply
myself I couldn't be any more lonely. If you
look carefully, there are many eyes gazing.
I wonder if all of this vigilance adds up
to kindness. I once saw a child on a train sleeping.

There was no guardian, no keeper
as she lay there breathing. If the eyes
are shut, what does our dreaming see?
The onlookers wondered where to place
the girl, wondered if they should wake
her or by doing so they would create a space
of abandon. Sometimes, my heart is an alarm clock
that wakes me to a startling sound. Sometimes
I rise in a museum of wandering objects
as the body imagines itself in pieces, fitted together,
roaming in a tangle of vanishing bloom.

ffffffffffoooooooooooouuuuuuuuuuurrrrrrrrrrrrrrrrrrrrrrrrrrr,
Sondra Perry

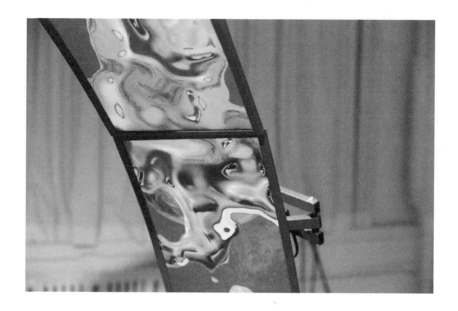

When I begin to drown, I sink to the very bottom.
I move my mouth, I mimic slow hunger.
I'm making a new world order, one
where the glass doesn't shatter, where
there is no surveillance. Everyone floats
except the ones who started the torrent,
the ones who laid the babies in watery graves,
then paddled away in a rowboat humming.
What is inside their song except a curse,
their bitter taste a contagion inside me.

I spit them out like seeds. Trees thrash the wind.
When the current turns I see an army of mothers
rooted on the other side, holding a legion
of future sons. Past and present mix and remix.
Media loops and plays in the muffled ambience.
When the floods come, I'll be ready, fire hot.
The surge melts when it touches me. Air, why
are you so wordless? Fire, why do you singe
everything called origin? Water, where did you
come from that you became my one true voice?
When I float face up, the lightning pulses
so far and untouchable, it refuses to be dead.

Woman Beneath a Woman, Kara Walker

Each breath makes me a billow, worn like rain
spiraling out into a vision of winter. If history
teaches me anything, it is of the vagaries
of burden. I can carry a vessel, a pitcher of water,
a bundle of ideas like sticks. I carry time like fire.
I hiccup and it's 2018 though the faces are the same:
Faces without faces and with different names.
If I run, the threat of a storm above
slows me. If I lift my arms, the rains
spill down. If I bend, my spine becomes
a terrain on which another treads. Sometimes,

I wish to unborn myself from this weather.
If I could walk out from under this thunder
there would be such air, my posture too
would lift. If I unborn myself, I'd give up
my sisters too, my brothers by the bridge,
so I'll stay lifting this largeness, this tonnage
of darkness, to live inside my cloud of kin.

DIVERSITY

The earth is full of giants who move time to stardust heaps.
      Each whip of a tail extends arms to reigns.

The word *backbreaking* comes from such litanies.
      The back is a light, a road overturned many times.

Song of selves. Sands move to overcome me. Others move
      to name the wind which has no name,

to leash me. What did God's hand hold without tension?
      What can a mind uncover without slipping through

the smallest of holes? A hole is an imagined shape.
      What it contains and its depth are often the same

unreachable dark. There were so many people naming themselves
      master, too many for me to hold a crown to dogs,

my arms tired from the weight of such feigned glory.
      Too many masters in the parlor, all of them

wishing to flood an entry with ideas and apology.
      Not wonder but longing, not mistake but caution,

not a whole but fractions, spent coins thud on the seabed.
      A body falls most often into a hole when others

aren't looking and what's the shape of that freefall?

TIMELINE FOR A BODY: 4 HOURS, 6 BULLETS

Once there was a body made with the blood
of me, days passed into the thirst of centuries
until a boy rose from born grasses, ether made,

spirited along the dirt, crossed from one path
to another. Nothing could make me think
there could ever be an end. Or maybe the contract

was, *I'll end first*. A body can be made voiceless,
made more object than spirit, more meat than wonder.
A body can be made heartless, driving back

into a corner where it's stripped of its pulsing
origin, honor. Some dream boys were etched
into tombstones long ago, gone gray.

~

Body to ground, hours stretch out, unfurled
to liquid, past police tape. Bullets formed a map
of a marksman's mind, storm inked onto its trajectory.

One day time will look exactly like a boy in the midst
of dreaming, shots which sounded like deep worry,
a body left alone, as chalk made its way along the street

in a stream that looked something like suspicion.
One day time will look exactly like this boy
and the many ways he could have been a man.

WAR CLOUD

I know they exist, from the bite marks trailing my leg,
my pack of hurt leopards roam far from here.

We live in a time when creatures do not name themselves.
The falcon ceases to be the carrier of messages.

The snail is no longer the harbinger of solitude. We are born
of many kingdoms, promise dressing a past wound.

If there could be such legacy, each room leads
to a larger room and each one we encounter leads us

to dreaming. I enter the woodlands to marry intention.
Right now, the bark are in the shape of wolves. Domesticated,

they curl at my ankles, ask for nothing. Guns line a walkway
leading to the past. Imagine: I place each foot down

on land mines, like paw prints on a river's face. It sounds
like glass breaking, a rush of voices after the floods.

The animals are coming. This time not two by two
but in swarms of rampage. We know them by their howling

which sound most human.

mongrel (n.)

late 15c., "mixed-breed dog," from obsolete *mong* "mixture,"
from Old English *gemong* "mingling" (base of *among*), from
Proto-Germanic *mangjan* "to knead together" (source of
mingle), from a nasalized form of PIE root *mag-* "to knead,
fashion, fit." With pejorative suffix *-rel*. Meaning "person not
of pure race" is from 1540s. As an adjective from 1570s.

BITCH

I found it encased in fur. Born and breathing, beast of one.

＊

It had been salivating at soul meat, seated on its haunches.

It lay by my feet looking upward. The stars drop from their celestial homes.

I stroke the muzzle, feed it. I imitate it, a living thing.

A beaming that, if one touches it, one could beam too.

⁑   ⁑

I look to the century, that seemed to name me, that seemed to call me both earth and shadow. A self-same widow.

✳

I could be ✳

a mutation, flowing back to the source.

✶ Laika

✶

Sputnik space dog

was the ultimate bitch.

A stray found on the streets of Moscow. Placed in a vessel.
Given oxygen and space food. Trained in the theory

of survival.

While humans went about their earth lives below, she remained chained but floating. Her canine self, a mortal wound.

How could she not love herself within that reflection?

Before her end?

Look now through a telescope.

It all is expelling. A radiant tide of unrest. All of my want fractured and escaping.

What do you see?

Now, I am unafraid to know. The field becomes wider and wider as if to summon me, to include me. To be adopted. To be housed.

Once upon a time, there were animals who possessed a master, who prodded them, pushing them to till the land, to shed their wool, to offer milk until the milk ran dry. Some called him shepherd, others not. He wielded a stick or a crook but no one called it a weapon. One day, the gates unlocked and a stampede ensued. The sheep and the horses ran and the shepherd fell, one by one they left their hoofprints in their fleeing. The dog stayed and sat next to him, licking from arm to fingertip as if the body was a map of unsolvable matter.

The female hounds behave fiercely to a lone female hound. I stand
outside the pack.

✳

✳

She never wanted anything from me but to call her one name, vital and direct, as if there was a charge between the one who calls out and her art.

"By 1930, the number of references that called a woman or women 'bitches' outnumbered those that referred to dogs."

"In the context of modern feminism, bitch has varied reappropriated meanings that may connote a *strong female . . . cunning . . .* or else it may be used as a tongue-in-cheek backhanded compliment for someone who has excelled in an achievement."

Laika was a she. Launched into orbit, tangled in a flight harness, a mongrel female.

*

I sometimes wake in the middle of the night and think there has been a theft of the mind. Along the way someone has taken a jewelry box away from me. In it there was my great desire wrapped in tissue paper, folded in felt encasing, and pulsating inside was the thing itself. My inclination was to think it was a garnet, or amulet, but more likely it was a word I had forgotten long ago, composed in shaky hand, a first word I wrote when I was a child. The first time I understood meaning. Word as breathing survivor.

The first living creature launched into orbit was a mixed breed she, crossing over. There was no reentry plan. The stars burned up with the heat that created them.

I sit at the base of the tree, low to the ground. Lower and the constellations seem to elevate and I am housed there. Dust particles filter through light. Fractured self hurtles, clouds of gas and dust gather under the might of gravity. The heat itself fuses into a sphere of fire at the beginning of time.

"You and I are made of stardust. We are the stuff of exploded stars. We are therefore at least one way that the Universe knows itself."

✳

If the soul is a living ember is it a fire that will not go out?

I must end on Laika whose name is derived from the word "barker"
which means you can fathom the open mouth

but you cannot hear the howl

AT THE END OF THE ROAD WAS A SUN

Once there were three children, all with different fates.
     One was bound to say yes all his life, head in books,
hand open for blistered discipline. When the slap
     came down, he looked out the window toward a country
he couldn't name. The second child spoke of the dream state
     where nothing could be held down; he headed out at morning,
worked till his sweat made an ocean of wonder, something blue
     but never forgotten. He was the wild earth, growing without limit
or reason. The third child ran away, writhed and cursed at history.
     He was nothing if not righteous. I can see him now, standing
in the field, ready to run but not ruin, ready to wrap his fists
     to throat to be free. I loved this son more than anything,
now my son no longer.

THEORY OF WAR

I made dioramas of the future: paper birds rested on live wire,
a sculpture of the sun rose like a mouth, then all the living
ones died magnificently inside the box. After that
there was song. Voices sprang out of the box with coil
and hinge. How the songs spoke and said they wanted nothing
but I listened until the sparks extinguished, until I could
sit beside the box and love it enough to close it.

~

I twisted the theory around my ankle like an anchor.
More like an ornament, jewelry I once loved. I wound it
around my leg, my bone loving the tension.
My children were there speaking into a hole
in a tree. So sweet, it haunted my future. Outside
there were guns. There were tanks. Outside
officers lifted skirts with the barrels of rifles.

~

I once walked the tightrope of history. The rope
made speeches. The rope swung with a hellfire of rants.
The rope said Halleluiah and raised its arms heavenward
and waved a handkerchief before dabbing its forehead
with its own belief and affliction. The rope watched
the followers in the pews faint. The rope was glad
for its power. It was a lowercase god. It was overcome
by itself. The windows of the chapel cracked
with the urgency of the great Lord in winter.

The rope had said it was a friend of the people
and followed it with *Amen*. The great doors blew suddenly open.
The rope held a rope. There was a tug of war and it won.

~

She wrote a book and called it *Aftermath*.
It was a large shelter made of ice, every object frozen
to its bereaved cold twin. The children loved her
when she told different endings to the same story
each time: The witch turned on herself, the witch
found herself among a pack of other witches,
the witch ate her hind leg to save herself from
the finality of death. The witch loved blood.
Each time the children gasped
and told her to tell the story again. She did so
willingly, opening a small shutter to her chest,
hearing a squeak and a tender clang. When she reset
the narrative once again, she readied herself
as if she would not be alive when the story ended.

A POEM CALLED POLITICS

When he was a boy
I tripped him.
It felt good
because the pallor
of his hand was a telescope
careening inside me.

I remember when
my knuckles skimmed
his teeth, his bite
broke skin but I took it
if it meant the tearing
where it felt best.

I wanted colossus
so I cradled the head,
tufts of hair falling
on my dark dress
strands making crossroads
on my night breast:
a trigger.

I called hate a bed
I could sleep in, a soft
resting place. *You lie,*
I say hard and close
into his puckered mouth
soulless, equal parts
foul and blubber.

I researched his kin,
feeble people with a capital F.
I fingered him behind the bushes
and when he was tall enough
to spit back at me, we tumbled
in the darkness that was blood.

When I unzipped his suit,
he was little buildings
with broken windows,
half-built shacks housed
a matchstick empire.

I see him now, firing
at the mountains. He says
the enemy is there
beyond the wall of clouds,
ephemeral, wistful.

It was like tearing
a Chinese painting
to pieces, smearing it
with dew, but more like
cutting open the sky,

no mercy on the sun's
slit face, no mercy
on its twin brother,
the moon, spilling

like an avalanche
of coins glittering
in a swampy bed.

FREEDOM GHAZAL

When the currency, vodka, arguments were done, I was free.
I searched for a name like a lost trinket blowing toward freedom.

I shall remain nameless, curled inside this nest, silent, withdrawn,
till the news is out: a revolution calling for freedom.

Never one to stop speaking, insists the telephone line.
It leans toward a neighboring pole, repeats speech's old freedom.

Oh hand, that causes me worry when the mouth hides my longing.
Oh foot, silence treks inside my shoe toward a foretold freedom.

My mother and father were sojourners along a black road,
only knew they should keep walking, a constant forward freedom.

What, reader, can I say so you would believe? What could I dream
that resembles the promised document of controlled freedoms?

I stand at the clock tower, the microphone, the wrong places
of speech and suicide, words come out wrong, bottomless freedom.

Sing me a song, I once ordered my lover, my bold desire
not a hammer, nor birds, nor fire, but a bare untouched freedom.

Come here, says the mother, *Little one, come here, dearest Roman.*
He places his head on my lap, the world unfolds its freedom.

VIVID ISOLATION

I lived in the past, coursed inside a tale in blood
Each fingerprint pressed into my false trail in blood.

Wide open the doors had blown, when students lay down
on streets to claim a signature that failed in blood.

Within my body, my father's race and speed bound
with fury, small wings, a boat bobbed in hail, in blood.

I had a child I hid from family, called *One*
a name he scripted on his tongue, *Love*, called his blood.

At night, I walked barefoot to another country
freed from my own conscience, found in kin, shared in blood.

Shahid died and folded a book into a bird,
released it East, it floated on saffron-scarred blood.

When does anyone arrive home, shoes off, coat hung,
through the door we walk, a refugee flagged in blood?

It's done, a land tilled for you. Agha, your imprint
is a couplet, tandem illusion, prayer in blood.

THE SHIFTING KINGDOM

Now there are only the cactus and the desert
blossoms unfolding their soft garments,

and the twilight road along whose crossings
dolls are strung in nettles, over whose skulls

prayers pass like a procession carrying cups
of wreckage. I am the runaway in a caravan

with no artillery. I had not thought enough of arrival,
of entering the portal of my mother's dream, of rising

from sleep with my cape of leaves and my mouth open—
like Jesus' robes—to bells and rampage,

trumpet and siren, and that song the horizon wails
just before dawn. Bodies left behind and the loss of it

forgotten. Now our hides are the coyote's shadow,
darker in our disappearance. My coat does not quite fit,

and the bleating ram will never bring me peace.
Here everyone obeys the coyote and no one knows

where to call, in whose belief to softly wade.
And in the desert sand the tale my grandmother

spoke to me, her voice floats over this worn pelt,
which no longer runs and shivers at his sound.

What I wished for is not as I understand it to be;
I have still not seen a savior, unless that warm wind

passing beyond the fences when my coyote
went for a walk was one. And though there are no exits,

no doorways or openings, there is also no way to enter.
There is only *God keep you* and *safekeeping.*

The roof blows away in the heat as barbed wire cuts
night wind. Here the girls lie down between tied ankles.

My fear is the unfurling road, with headlights searing
and no sleep in sight. It is a back that bends to the gruel

of my ancestor's song, a reminder of kitchen hands
like dying coal, a country that is a splinter of a shelter.

276

1.1 Hausa Tongue

Burning, it was clear: A call, herdsman
Hours later trucks and buses. Thrust
And a wave, splashed onto every corner of world,
Global Wail, observer fear, evil by its name. Wives
Of the Lord's Resistance. Spectrum of gold, trade,
Thrive, trace amounts. Hoodwinked, paradise,
Low level, tides. Faraway, no country Untouched.

2.2 Boko Haram

Educational gunpoint. Slim-less authority.
Grueling struck. Poor-Kind archetype.
Woo the same man. Woo Chibok girls. Woo Woo.
Nothing interception, into the fray. Cement, sugar, salt.
Movie industry, Nollywood. Pimp family for sugar.
Islamic coverings, Faith. Allah. Woo. Boko Thuggery.

2.3 Operative Across Country VIII

Law-enforcement, commercial satellite, flying
Manned reconnaissance missions
Missing girls. Lost forever—and be.

3.1 Song of the Checkered Dress

I chortled this hausa hausa's minion, burning-
　　Dome of rooflight's rage, raining-roar-ravage Eagle, in his turning
　　Of the running bride-maid gasoline air, and churning
Wives there, how she piled upon the flatbed of a truck's clearing
In her chastity, then on, on forth, on crowing,
　　As a slave's heel digs on a road's end: the girl and herding
　　Tufted the big cloud. My trade in gurgling:
Coin for a lion, dominant of, the taming of the thing!

Rouged beauty, enslaven and sell, oh, heir, thrive, throne, here
　　Marriage! AND the flame that collapses from thee, company
Threading less holier, more damaged, O my children!

　　No evidence of it: sheer boko makes bough down symphony
Glitter, and ruby-radiant tinder, ah my wren,
　　Twitter chill-cacophony, squeal themselves. Hatch.

DEVIL

And it was here that I fell down a great depth.
    Lord, will you wake me? Say Death
and I say how deep? Say Hell and I say
    which one? There were many circles
to this waking, many ways to stand
    so the spine cracked and rebuilt itself
into a canyon. Can't say the body didn't try.
    Can't say the mouth and the esophagus
didn't ring with hellfire, didn't do their duty.

I said I was sorry until the words piled up
    in graves, in sanctuary.
Every time I made my peace with peace,
    it turned on me. It folded the paper in half
and crossed out a treaty with red silk.
    Lord, I made my peace, but the Devil
is still here. *It doesn't matter,* says the Devil,
    how good you were. It's just a shadow
of an outcry, a little kindling to throw

in the campfire of doubt. He says, *Little One,*
    do not be so lonely. He says, *Lamb, eat the grass.*
Now bend. Now go deeper. Once I stepped backward,
    a hinge unlocked and there was a caravan
of fire which rolled down a hill. Once
    I woke, there were five furious men
standing on grass. If I took to the field,
    they ran after me. If I stood still, they magnified.
If I hid behind a canvas of trees, they found me

camouflaging as one of the few maples.

 I stood rooted, then flamed. That was the only way
to live: Burn it down. When everything rose up,

 I looked back and saw all my faces
and all my guises fall away to smoke.

 Do you think you're in a fairy tale?
Do you think you've become the last fallen fruit?

FEVER GHAZAL

Here is a place that was once mine, each grown flower a fever
reaches through a gate, now flourishes like a wounded fever.

The body was once a compass leading due North. When it broke
I could say I was lost or free. Each step a hounded fever.

When he sleeps, my son is neither broken nor compromised,
his body a road leading to a house of spoon-fed fever.

My nation speaks stories into my mouth as if they were mine.
Are they document, aftermath? The news a clouded fever.

What if the story told has no clear beginning and no end?
When the compass cracks, the dial is a floundering fever.

If we move quickly from one room to another we miss it.
We search for it in the kitchen, first known fire, last found fever.

Matches struck by the light of your weary hand, America,
papers burned in the quickening gold, God's mind crowned in fever.

BURIAL, A LULLABY

I asked to be buried inside my son
once all was done. The living.
People thought it odd, this level
of loyalty and then I saw the birds
circling in arcs over coffins.

How to be buried before dead?
How to tuck oneself into a knot
inside a knot? How to die
before death and exist beside
the living?

There are objects within objects
all the time, some of them are human.
Let some of them be human.
Let some of them multiply.
There is a misshapen seed inside
the ground. Grown, when fathered.

PROPHECY

I will strike down white caps of longing on which the boats sail, Mama
I will strike down the buildings in which reside clouds of ammunition,
I will explode the vicissitudes of hatred, armed guards
with jagged swords, with shields in the name of patience,
where cowardice is brandished in handcuffs, Mama
where the brute force of discipline is placed in whose hands,
strike down anything with a vein for bleeding and a shock of hair,
strike down by not striking, the baton breaks the head parts, Mama
when you had a mouth, you used to speak, Mama
strike down the hammer, the hammer strikes down
the heart pushes back, resuscitates, Mama

I reject walls and those who build them, Mama
I reject the safety of fear,
I reject salvation in the form of nourishment, Mama

Make room for the rising undercurrent
which will carry us to bloom, Mama
Make room for the resurgence of bliss that once filled your cup
Make room for men who say their name is grace or mercy, Mama
what they mean is root and chain
what they mean is organization as force
what they mean is tangle and barbed wire
prison is what they mean, Mama

I can bet you that language is not their own,
I can bet their tongues unfurl themselves at night
when their mouths sag in repose
when the mouth is no longer a hound, when the mouth

rests unworthy like a leash
sometimes that leather tears, Mama
I can say now, words were once teeth, Mama
I break my expectations when the bone is broken,
yet another man lost at sea, before that
back, neck, spine cracked, matters of discipline
the tufted fur skims the sidewalk, Mama

It was never discipline enough to say, Yes
Never broken enough to say, No
We ride now toward the last kingdom, Mama
Dark immigrant face, heart dissolved to a berry,
then shrunken to seed but don't be fooled
when nothing grows, Mama

I was birthed here. I'm alone, Mama

Today I shall write one line that continues
to the end of the world
and in so doing I have faced the wound, Mama

Wound is the world with its hair on fire
Once fresh, there was my boyhood, Mama
I can say I'm older now and to say that
I mean it is real and I can face it, Mama

Say it now: The Future

Black boot, black boot, black boot
Black boot, black boot, black boot
Black boot, black boot, black boot
Black boot, black boot, black boot
Black boot, black boot, black boot

March, march, march

Black boot, black boot, black boot
Black boot, black boot, black boot
Black boot, black boot, black boot
Black boot, black boot, black boot
Black boot, black boot, black boot

March, march

Black boot,
Black boot,
Black boot,
Black boot,
Black boot,
Black boot,

Black boot
Black
Boot

March

My boots are a prophecy.
A future hurricane.
I was a boy. A man.
A father. A god.
I chisel no headstones.
I'll never turn back.

COLOR

Up ahead it's white. Snow animal,
I'm running at your back. I've failed to tell you
I've been hungry all this time, to tell you
I've been searching for you, like meat,
like water. All my life, I've distanced
myself. As if to know you was to drown.
As if to find you I'd usher myself further
from what is real. I've been adrift along
the threads of time leading me out
beyond an imagined frame. I've untied myself,
uncuffed the arms and neck. I didn't know
I was hurt like that. I didn't know
there was a force pulling me downward
toward bedrock, lulling me to sleep.
You are the one escaping, you are the one
breaking free. I understand your astonishing
dash to freedom, done with the estranged wind,
done with frost and storm, orchids curling
outward beyond grief. The road widens
to glory. The road disappears.

§

I come back in the secret room
slip into a skin
and walk out
blended in with the world.

EYE

RECOGNITION

WHO AM I

— ROMAN

ACKNOWLEDGMENTS

My gratitude to the following journals and anthologies in which versions of these poems first appeared:

The Academy of American Poets' Poem-a-Day: "Fury" and "Astroturf"

Brooklyn Poets Anthology, edited by Jason Koo and Joe Pan, Brooklyn Arts Press: "4 Portraits"

The Eloquent Poem anthology, edited by Elise Paschen, Persea Books: "Vivid Isolation"

The Kiss anthology, edited by Brian Turner, W. W. Norton & Company: "Revolutionary Kiss"

Liberation: New Works on Freedom from Internationally Renowned Poets, edited by Mark Ludwig, Beacon Press: "276"

PEN America: A Journal for Writers & Readers, *Mythologies* issue: "Timeline for a Body: 4 Hours, 6 Bullets"

Triquarterly: "Patience" and "Prophecy"

Two Countries: US Daughters & Sons of Immigrant Parents anthology, edited by Tina Schumann, Red Hen Press: "The Shifting Kingdom"

The Virginia Quarterly Review: "He, Pronoun," "Creation Myth," and "Color"

Writing Motherhood, A Creative Anthology, edited by Carolyn Jess-Cooke, Seren Books: "Milk"

"Bitch" was written for artist Jessica Rankin's solo installation where poets produced poems and a publication that responded to her show. Poetry for this showcase was curated by the poet Brenda Shaughnessy.

Parts of "Hybrida: A Zuihitsu" first appeared in an interview called "A Complex Collision of Selves," conducted by Theresa Sullivan for the Garrison Institute.

My heartfelt thanks to Tracy K. Smith, my first primary reader, collaborator, and partner in all things Magick. For her immovable love and devotion, Amy Brill, and to Jennifer Milich for being my truest heart. My gratitude to Audrey Peterson for her vision and perspective as well as Peter Covino and Robin Beth Schaer for their close and sensitive reading of the book-in-progress. I am honored to have had the support, inspiration, and creative sustenance from the following people: Emily Abt, Raphael Allison, Harry Barrick, Julian Bevan, Ben Cruz, Matthew Dickman, Rachel Eliza Griffiths, Kimiko Hahn, Nathalie Handal, Terrance Hayes, Lara Held, Marie Howe, Paolo Javier, Charlotta Koehler, Michele Kotler, Donna Masini, Kamilah Aisha Moon, Brian Morton, Gregory Pardlo, Camryn Prince, Roger Reeves, Martha Rhodes, Nicole Sealey, Sreshtha Sen, Vijay Seshadri, Charif Shanahan, Ravi Shankar, Brenda Shaughnessy, Holly Wren Spalding, Craig Morgan Teicher, Melissa Walsh, Jacqueline Woodson, Xu Xi. To my dear teachers, Agha Shahid Ali, Lucie Brock-Broido, Arthur Clements, Lucille Clifton, Constance Coiner, Alfred Corn, Mark Doty, David Lehman, Richard Locke, Alice Quinn, Ruth Stone. I remember each line of magic, every lesson. My admiration to the following organizations for the immense work they do and my gratitude for their support: The Academy of American Poets, Asian American Writers' Workshop,

Aspen Words, Brooklyn Poets, Cave Canem, Kundiman, Pen Parentis, Poetry Foundation, Poetry Society of America, Poets House, Singapore Unbound, Still Waters in a Storm, The Community-Word Project, Urban Word NYC, 92nd Street Y. Thanks to the Blue Flower Arts team for their attention to every detail, every delicate nuance. My continued gratitude to the Blue Mountain Center where many of these poems were written over a number of residencies and Four Way Books who gave me voice and home. A nod to the many students who have journeyed along with me, especially my family of *hybrid beasts*. A very special thanks to Lara Rosenthal whose most individual, selfless, enduring generosity sheltered me while I wrote this book. To my mother, Teresa Lee, who offered me every beautiful gift in this world, with her own brand of grace, thank you. My heartfelt and humble appreciation to Sondra Perry, Alexandria Smith, Kara Walker, Kehinde Wiley, and the artists with whom I find collaboration here.

My immense gratitude to Jill Bialosky for her leadership and faith in me. I thank Drew Elizabeth Weitman for her patience and delicacy in all matters, and the amazing W. W. Norton team for just about everything.

My love to all of my families, especially my most essential family: Claude, Juliette, and Roman.

NOTES

The YouTube video in "Creation Myth" is of Kametra Barbour who was driving home in Forney, Texas, on August 9, 2014, with four children under the age of ten. She was stopped and handcuffed by police officers who were responding to a dispatch. They were searching for four men in a beige or tan Toyota. Ms. Barbour's car was a burgundy Nissan Maxima. Her son emerging from the car was six years old at the time.

Michael Brown's angelic vision is a quote from the article, "Michael Brown Spent Last Weeks Grappling With Problems and Promise," by John Eligon, *New York Times*, August 24, 2014. The quote by Lesley McSpadden is from the article "For the Family of Michael Brown, Grief, Sorrow and Anger Play Out in Public Eye," by DeNeen L. Brown, *Washington Post*, December 1, 2014.

"Mankind is so Fallible" is a title after Heather Altfield. The poem draws from the Charleston church shooting. On June 17, 2015, Dylann Roof, a twenty-one-year-old white supremacist, walked into the Emanuel African Methodist Episcopal Church in South Carolina during prayer service and shot and killed nine people including the church's senior pastor. The church was 202 years old at the time and has a significant place in black history from support during the slavery era, to the Civil Rights Movement, to Black Lives Matter.

The poem "Milk" was inspired by the life of Leiby Kletzky who was an eight-year-old Hasidic Jewish boy. Kletzky was kidnapped while walking home from day camp on June 11, 2011. His body was found two days later in the Kensington apartment of Levi Aron and also in a dumpster in Sunset Park. Leiby had asked his parents if he could walk home alone instead of taking the school bus. His parents honored his wish after practicing the route home many times. Upon leaving camp, Leiby missed a turn and headed in the wrong direction.

The source of the definitions of *hybrid* and *mongrel* are derived from www.etymonline.com.

"Timeline for a Body: 4 Hours, 6 Bullets," takes its name partially from the *New York Times* article "Timeline for a Body, 4 Hours in the Middle of a Ferguson Street" by Julie Bosman and Joseph Goldstein and an accompanying video segment called "Michael Brown's Body" by Brent McDonald and Alexandra Garcia, published on August 23, 2014. On August 9, 2014, Michael Brown was fatally shot by police officer Darren Wilson and his body was left on the pavement for four hours in view by neighbors, bystanders, relatives, and children, before his body was removed. Michael Brown, unarmed, was eighteen years old.

The poem "Bitch" is inspired by Laika, a stray dog, one of the first animals to be launched into orbit on the spacecraft *Sputnik 2*. The poem contains a number of quotes:

page 86: from "You Say 'Bitch' Like It's a Bad Thing, Examining the Implications of the Notorious Word," by Zoë Triska, *Huffington Post*, January 23, 2013, updated December 6, 2017.

page 87: via Wikipedia: "Pop Goes the Feminist," Deborah Solomon interview of Andi Zeisler, *New York Times*, August 6, 2006; "Third Wave Feminism," by Tamara Straus, MetroActive, December 6, 2000;

"You've Really Got Some Minerva, Veronica Mars," archived 2007-04-23 at the Wayback Machine, 2006-11-21.

page 92: Bill Nye to Reddit, November 5, 2014, https://www.reddit.com/r/IAmA/comments/2le34s/bill_nye_undeniably_back_ama/.

"The Shifting Kingdom" is after Brigit Pegeen Kelly's poem "Lost in the Peaceable Kingdom." The poem draws from the life of Noemi Álvarez Quillay, who attempted to journey 6,500 miles from the southern highlands of Ecuador to New York City, where her mother and father lived. Accompanied by coyotes, human smugglers, and one month after her departure she was picked up in Mexico by the authorities and taken to a children's shelter. A few days later she was found hanged from a shower-curtain rod. Authorities ruled it a suicide. She was twelve years old.

Many of the fragments of "276" are quotes from "The Modern Slave Trade" by Belinda Luscombe, *Time* magazine, May 15, 2014. The title "276" comes from the number of girls who were taken from their dormitories in Chibok, Nigeria, on April 14, 2014. Section 3.1 is after Gerard Manley Hopkins's poem, "The Windhover."

"Prophecy" is a poem after Donald Hall's poem with the same title.

ILLUSTRATION CREDITS

page 53: Kehinde Wiley (American, born 1977). *Napoleon Leading the Army over the Alps*, 2005. Oil on canvas, 108 × 108 in. (274.3 × 274.3 cm). Collection of Brooklyn Museum, Partial gift of Suzi and Andrew Booke Cohen in memory of Ilene R. Booke, and in honor of Arnold L. Lehman, Mary Smith Dorward Fund, and William K. Jacobs Jr. Fund, 2015.53. © Kehinde Wiley. Courtesy: Sean Kelly, New York.

page 55: Alexandria Smith / "go run tell dat" / 16 × 20 in. / collage on board / 2013. Courtesy Alexandria Smith.

page 57: *fffffffffffooooooooooooouuuuuuuuuurrrrrrrrrrrrrrrrrrrrrr-rrrrr* video and bicycle workstation, dimensions variable. Installation for "Sick Time, Sleepy Time, Crip Time: Against Capitalism's Temporal Bullying," Elizabeth Foundation for the Arts Project Space, 2017. Photo Credit: Matthew Vicari. © Sondra Perry.

page 59: Kara Walker. *Emancipation Approximation, Scene #18*, 2000. Screenprint. 44 × 34 inches (111.8 × 86.4 cm). © Kara Walker, courtesy of Sikkema Jenkins & Co., New York.

page 81: Courtesy Felix Mittermeier.

TINA CHANG is the Poet Laureate of Brooklyn and the first female to be named to this role. Raised in New York City, she is the author of the collections of poetry *Of Gods & Strangers* (2011) and *Half-Lit Houses* (2004). She is also the co-editor of the W. W. Norton anthology *Language for a New Century: Contemporary Poetry from the Middle East, Asia, and Beyond* (2008). In 2011, she was awarded The Women of Excellence Award for her outreach and literary impact on the Brooklyn community. In 2014 and 2017, *Brooklyn Magazine* named Chang one of the 100 Most Influential People in Brooklyn Culture. Her work often brings her to international audiences in China, Singapore, Hong Kong, among many other parts of the world. Chang is the recipient of awards from the New York Foundation for the Arts, Academy of American Poets, *Poets & Writers*, the Ludwig Vogelstein Foundation, and the Van Lier Foundation among others. Tina Chang received her MFA in poetry from Columbia University. She teaches poetry at Sarah Lawrence College and was also a member of the international writing faculty at the City University of Hong Kong. She lives in Brooklyn with her family.